RUGBY WORLD CUP 2007

RUGBY WORLD CUP 2007

RUGBY!

(WHAT RUGBY?)

Compiled by
Roger Entwistle

ARTHUR H. STOCKWELL LTD.
Torrs Park Ilfracombe Devon
Established 1898
www.ahstockwell.co.uk

First published in Great Britain, 2007

British Library Cataloguing-in-Publication Data.
A catalogue record for this book is available from the British Library.

Arthur H. Stockwell Ltd. bears no responsibility for the accuracy of events recorded in this book.

ISBN 978-0-7223-3816-2
Printed in Great Britain by
Arthur H. Stockwell Ltd.
Torrs Park Ilfracombe
Devon

This book is dedicated to all those Old Croydonians and Croydon R.F.C., past and present, without whom this book would not have been possible. A special thanks to all who contributed stories: Brian Hodges, Ian Sorrell, Taffy Smith, Eddie Jones, Mark Gartland and Anon. Also John Davies for the archives. Illustrations by Mike Komarnyckyj.

Thanks for some wonderful memories.

Semper Recordemur

Egon Rontwistle

Contents

ISLE OF WIGHT EASTER TOUR

"Where the bloody hell's Sorrell got to?"

Any member of the general public passing Croydon Town Hall on Good Friday morning could have heard the plaintive cry. The rest of our tour party had assembled virtually on time, and the only one late was the man who organised the whole thing – our 'leader', Ian Sorrell. But he does have to come all the way from New Addington, someone pointed out (New Addington being only a mile or so from Croydon). Then, through the early morning smog, exactly thirty-six minutes and three seconds late, full of bullshit and excuses, the great man arrived and the tour was under way.

Having stopped to pick up Roger "I've got an E-Type" Entwistle, who, along with a few others, set the tone for the tour by getting straight on the piss, we learned that Tony Porter had become a father at last (and so dispelling those ugly rumours about his sperm count).

Someone then suggested that a small whip-round be taken to replenish the stocks. (Roger had already drunk two thirds of the booty himself and the coach had only gone five miles.) So up jumps D. Macintosh Esquire, who relieved us of another couple of quid each and proceeded to stop the coach at the nearest off licence. Within ten minutes he's back with twenty-five pipkins, two crates of light ale, a crate of Guinness and enough pork pies to feed an army; and we are on our way once more.

On reaching Portsmouth, we had a few minutes to spare

before loading the boat, so we decided to use up the remainder of the whip-round savouring the local brew – Brickwoods Bitter. This was unanimously voted the worst beer in the world, and it was with great effort that pints were downed so we could board the ferry and get to the bar.

Now, the merits of Old Croydonians RFC as a singing club may have been a disputable point up until the start of the tour. However, the somewhat tepid renderings on the coach between Croydon and Portsmouth gave way to a series of full-throated numbers in the ferry's bar. It was here that that little chubby darling, John "Where's my baby powder?" Marshall, gave us all a taste of things to come, when, uninhibited by the great British public, he performed the first strip of the tour.

Sometime during the ferry crossing, Paul Sorrell managed to find a beer barrel which, by the way he was struggling with it, seemed full. But, unfortunately, it turned out to be empty. It was carried undauntedly to the coach to become our first trophy of the tour.

On reaching the hotel, a rather quaint piece of Sorrell tour management came to light when it was discovered that certain members of the tour party had to share double beds. Those fortunate enough to select the lucky room keys were Dave Hambridge and Fred Allen, Doug Macmillan and Brian Hodges, and Tony Porter and John Marshall. (It should be noted that out of four men who were to share John Marshall's room, and who were destined to lie between the same sheets, it was only he who most unselfishly insisted that he wouldn't mind sharing!)

With everyone settled in, the bar was opened, dinner was ordered and Roger Entwistle was sick, blaming the Brickwoods Bitter, of course!

That evening saw the first excursion to one of the island's night spots – a booming loud discotheque. The hunt was then on for the local crotch, with varying degrees of success: most people got at least one dance and one refusal and ended up pissed.

Terry Barret staked his claim for the 'ugliest bird' award by picking up (figuratively, of course – physically it would have been impossible) a fair young maiden who could have graced the front row of a London Welsh 1st XV.

This visit drew to a rapid close when Barry Chandler, having reached his mischievous mood, hurled the remnants of his beer into the air. This resulted in John Butterworth throwing half a pint over Pete Gill, who, not to be outdone, crowned the aggro of the scene by hurling a full pint back over John and anyone stood within fifteen feet of him.

A hasty retreat was beaten back to the hotel with two taxis full of birds in tow so that the serious business of drinking (Roger was about to get pissed for the third time that day) and singing good old rugby songs was got down to. (Various other things were also got down to that night, which probably accounts for the abortive game on Saturday afternoon.)

The breakfast room in the hotel on the Saturday morning after the Friday night before took on a distinctly sombre tone, with tender stomachs, bloodshot eyes and thumping heads, having to cope with fried eggs, fried tomatoes, fried bacon, fried sausages, fried mushrooms, and fried bread, not to mention the odd wet fart emulating from Roger.

Whilst the keener members of the tour strolled along Shanklin Pier, taking in the fresh air and sunshine, a rather select group retired to the pub for an impromptu lunchtime piss-up.

Later that afternoon we played our first match against the Hurricanes – a side only beaten three times that season – and, despite a continual barrage of insults and comments issued by the drunken partnership of Chandler and Entwistle on the touchline, strengthened by the arrival of Howard Cooper and Roger Heywood, we turned on a scintillating performance to win 19–11.

The shock of seeing Old Croydonians playing like a rugby side was too much for skipper Andy Nixon, who promptly contracted flu after the game, rendering him poorly. He could only sit and watch as the festivities got under way again and the boozing began in earnest. Although the drinking and singing were of fine quality, the evening definitely belonged to one Barry Chandler, who performed one of the most amazingly dainty strips you could feast your eyes upon. Unfortunately, our little performer seemed quite overcome by his new-found talents: by the end of the evening, he had collapsed into a chair, which then collapsed on him as he was carried to the awaiting coach.

We departed for the Hurricane's clubhouse, leaving quite a favourable impression and about £40's worth of damage, including twenty-eight unpaid-for pints and the remnants of a football table upon which Roger had insisted on using a pickled onion for a ball.

During the rest of Saturday evening, some people retired early to bed, others returned to the previous night's hunting ground and some just got pissed again (no prizes for guessing who).

The Sabbath dawned bright and clear, and, after a quiet morning of cards, draughts and shandies, we all rushed around like blue-arsed flies to catch the coach to our next match in good time for the 1.30 kick-off. Now, whether our opponents, J. S. White, purposefully put forward the kick-off time to 3.00 just so we would end up in the local pub drinking for an hour and a half (which we did!), or whether Sorrell is just a disorganised bastard, still remains a mystery.

We eventually kicked off with a slightly weaker side than the previous day's but, despite a spirited display by some of the players from the lower sides, we lost 6–3. This result was slightly unfair to us as such a good performance was made by players from the lower sides of the club, who all without exception played to a high standard.

The events of Sunday evening made it, by general consent, the best of the tour. On the face of it, a trip to a quiet country pub seems quite innocent but when one takes into account a free-flowing beer supply, a crowd of progressively less sober blokes, a hoard of cheery locals and a series of bawdy songs culminating in all eighty-three verses of 'The Wild West Show' from the husky baritone duo of John Huxtable and

Paul Sorrell, it becomes easy to understand why even the most liberal of landlords breathed a sigh of relief when we departed.

On returning to the hotel, the party got into full swing, and as my recollections of the night's revelry are muddled, to say the least, especially their chronological order, I shall simply list those occurrences which I can remember:

Dave Hambridge swigging on a bottle of Pernod – "Well, it's only money."

Everybody removing their trousers and parading around the hotel in various stages of undress.

Throwing Ian Sorrell naked into the sea!

Throwing Bert into the sea!

Roger throwing up into the sea!

John Butterworth proving himself right – farts do light up!

Barry Chandler performing the inevitable strip on the bar right in front of the barmaid, who was trying very hard not to take a good look!

John Marshall, John Savage and Tony Pollard finding their bed clothes all over the floor.

John Marshall, John Savage and Tony Pollard throwing Doug Macmillan onto the floor and nearly suffocating him under a mattress for wrecking their bedding!

Bert admitting to it later!

And the brilliant shower of sparks which followed a cushion being hurled by one of our number into a large chandelier.

Our last morning saw a general cramming of suitcases, tidying of rooms and collecting of soiled socks and dirty pants from under the beds. Plans were then laid for a final piss-up at a pub our good old tour manager knew of. After all his other cock-ups, it came as no surprise to us that, on arriving at the pub, we found the bloody thing had closed years ago. So, undaunted, we took over the alehouse next door. A tremendous singing session ensued, with everyone consuming as much beer as the previous three days would allow. It must be recorded here that this festive occasion was the only time during the tour that our club captain could be

John Marshall, John Savage and Tony Pollard throwing Doug Macmillan onto the floor and nearly suffocating him under a mattress.

seen a trifle inebriated – they must have put too much sherry in the trifle, Andy!

Having obtained the attention and applause of the locals (one of whom assured us he had only nipped in for a pee and ended up staying for two and a half hours), sung all our songs, and been treated to a solo by what must have been one of the bravest birds on the island (she stood up in the midst of thirty lechering, leering, pissed blokes and watched Entwistle perform the last strip of the tour), we thanked the landlord for staying open an extra forty minutes after hours and legged it back to the hotel, where we all said our goodbyes to a very relieved hotelier.

We unfortunately, due to the exploits of some of our squad on a go-cart track, missed the next ferry to Portsmouth and were forced to take refuge in the British Rail bar for an hour. However, we finally set sail with Ian Glassington, sensing the tour was at an end, trying desperately one more time to get his oats with a bird who, quite frankly, looked like anyone's final bid. All poor Ian got for his woes was a quick squint at her red knickers – and that was only with the help of the rest of us.

So the tour was at an end. We made the final leg from Portsmouth to Croydon and, although Barry and Roger tried their best to keep us all amused, they soon shut up when no one was listening. Most were asleep, and everyone was exhausted – except Ian Sorrell, who wouldn't stop whingeing, and Tubby Marshall, who was putting all his effort into maintaining his position as the most aggravating git of the tour. Even the plan to stop at a pub on the journey home was abandoned.

We then made a detour to Banstead, for no apparent reason other than to drop Roger "The Puker" Entwistle home. Eventually we made it home to Croydon, where it all broke up after a most enjoyable four days, either to go home to bed or, if you were Ian Sorrell, to try to find your car that had been nicked!

(Divine retribution?)

ROTTERDAM BY STORM

When one considers how long it's taken Great Britain to obtain entry into the Common Market, it seems ridiculous that thirty-five people could have reversed that Brussels agreement and ruined all the goodwill in just a matter of four days.

It was my fault I suppose. We should never have met in The Catherine Wheel pub two hours before we boarded the coach on that Good Friday lunchtime. The coach driver, poor misguided fool that he was, said there was to be no drinking on the bus. This statement was rendered useless after Dave Mac had promised to do something with an empty beer can that would have resulted in a very uncomfortable journey for the poor hapless chap unless he promised to change his mind. We soon got under way!

After what seemed an interminable wait at Luton Airport, we finally saw our plane arrive. Some of the weaker members of our party started to cry and shake whilst others fell into a stunned silence. The plane, a Dakota something or another, seemed as though it had just been dragged out of the Imperial War Museum. It was hardly worthy of carrying passengers, let alone flying to Holland. However, things did get worse. Firstly, all our luggage wouldn't fit, then they couldn't find any one brave enough to put the petrol in, and then, to top it all, they couldn't find the bloody pilot!

We eventually took our lives in our hands and had the courage to board. The hostess, bless her, greeted us warmly just as a drop of rain came through the roof. Amid cheers, cries of anguish and the sound of Roger being sick again, we took off. I won't say the thing flew low, but if the North Sea had been a bit choppier, the waves would have knocked us out of the sky.

On arrival at Rotterdam a short delay ensued because Peter Gill had done his usual trick of packing his passport in his suitcase. We were then met in arrivals by a member of the Rotterdam RFC and driven to our hotel, where a very bewildered manager informed us that he would be locking the doors at 2.30 each night. Some people just love to make life difficult for themselves.

The night was spent drinking in various bars around the city, and the extent of the drunkenness was best witnessed by the pools of sick outside the players' rooms and trails of it on the stairs the following morning.

Our first game against Rotterdam was a scrappy affair, to say the least, but we still won 16–6. The evening was spent in drunken debauchery with our hosts in the bar next to the hotel where Pat Cornan fell in love with a lady called Boopy. She was old enough to be his mother but her main attribute was that she didn't mind her female parts being fondled, jostled, jolted, caressed, stroked, pushed, poked or rolled around by all and sundry.

Ian Glassington, who managed to stay in a permanently pissed state the whole tour, had now become a fluent speaker of Dutch, rendering him completely incomprehensible.

The wonderful thing about Dutch bars is that they open at 9.00 a.m. This meant that on Sunday most of us were pissed by 10.30 and this set the stage for possibly the best day of the tour. We played against Te Weuve, the Royal Dutch Shell side and won 48–0 – a really splendid open game. In the evening, we had a colossal booze-up with Huxtable and Hambridge doing an excellent rendition of 'Old Macdonald's Farm'.

Considering we did about £50 worth of damage to the clubhouse, the Dutch were really friendly and took it all in good part. Entwistle hit his peak on this occasion and performed magnificently on the children's playground in front of a crowd of quizzical onlookers. After we had been refused entry to a posh dinner dance held by the Te Weuve Hockey Club, we decided to leave. Unfortunately we had lost Jean Glassington by this time with some strange foreign illness. (There you are, Jean, I told you I wouldn't tell everyone you got as pissed as the rest of us!)

Before we returned to Rotterdam, we decided to pay a visit to a country bar. A seventeen-man scrummage accounted for most of the damage, I suppose, although one or two surly individuals did their part. Needless to say, the landlord was quite happy to order us a fleet of taxis to take us away.

I feel that at this point I must point out that John Savage lost his virginity that night, and was the only person on the tour to do so. Unfortunately for him, the hotel manager, who had been awakened no less than eight times the previous night, had flatly refused to let *anyone* out of the hotel after 1.00 a.m. What she told her husband we'll never know, but I hope it was all worth it, John.

Monday dawned, and as soon as we'd packed we just had time to spend three or four hours in the bar. Then we were off to The Hague to play our last match of the tour.

The Hague are the current Dutch champions and their side contained no less than six Dutch internationals (or Dutch caps, as Roger put it). Our lads, a ragbag mixture of all four Croydonian sides, put up a terrific display only to lose 21–16. Still, a good time was had by all and we were soon back off to Rotterdam Airport in time for the 9.00 p.m. take-off. The only problem was, Air Anglia thought it was a 7.00 p.m. take-off. By the time we had rounded everyone up from the bogs, the customs, the duty-free and the bar we eventually left at 9.30 p.m. Needless to say, the crew were not too enamoured with us, but the worst was yet to come.

Anybody who goes on tour with Old Croydonians is bound to feel embarrassed at one time or another. At Luton Airport, I, for one, would have crawled into a corner and hidden if the scene was not so hilarious. Briefly, we arrived at about 11.00 p.m. and in the reception lounge were about seven to eight hundred normal, peace-loving, law-abiding respectable Easter holidaymakers returning home from wherever. In a short time there was pandemonium. Old Croydonians were back! screaming and bawling like banshees, having luggage-trolley races through the hall, singing rugby songs as loudly as possible and chasing as many air hostesses as would dare venture in sight. We were then rounded up like a flock of sheep by the airport police, roped off and made to wait until all the other people had cleared customs.

We were eventually released after much annoyance and made our weary way home after a further delay whilst John Collomosse insisted on being strip-searched by an aggravated customs official. But we were soon herded out to our coach and eventually arrived back at Croydon Town Hall to disperse to our homes.

All I can say is that if that's life in the Common Market, why the hell did it take so long to get in?

. . . whilst John Collomosse insisted on being strip-searched by an aggravated customs official.

YORK, GATEWAY TO THE NORTH

We had been at the hotel for a mere ninety seconds when Ian Sorrell managed to incur the wrath of the owners. He was found in the bar, serving pints to all and sundry. Mr Sorrell's estimate of the round pulled as "One pint and two halves, luv" was quickly shot down in flames by the fact that at least ten big lads had freshly pulled pints! Ian's haste to serve can only be explained by the fact that British Rail had managed to reserve us seats on a train, crossing half the British Isles, that didn't have a buffet coach. It was only Ian that failed to cater for such an eventuality, as the rest of the tour party had brought their own. In fact, Dave Usher's suitcase was found on further examination to contain one pair of socks, one pair of pants and a toothbrush; the rest of it was filled with enough booze to float the Royal Navy.

Having therefore endured a somewhat spartan journey from King's Cross – no more than eight pints per head – we booked into the hotel, leaving Sorrell to make good the round, boarded a coach and set off to Pocklington. Here we made a triumphant entrance and a dramatic exit from the local seven-a-side tournament.

By now, all but the unfortunate seven who had taken part in the game had reached the advanced state of inebriation, and soon it was up to the Old Croydonians to start the singing. Hambridge was, of course, well to the fore with a number of throaty, not to say timely, renditions. But the evening will always be Pat Cornan's, especially with his excellent impersonation of Gary Glitter. Sporadically during the weekend, brief snatches of this treat were to be re-enacted, but they were all shadows of the hilarious original for which Pat, shy and unassuming introvert that he is, will no doubt always be remembered.

On returning to York, we poured out of the bus and straight into a Berni Inn, managing to ruin Good Friday for both clientele and staff of this establishment. Whilst most of the party were gainfully occupied in hurling bread rolls at one another, or playfully rolling empty wine bottles under precariously balanced waitresses, Cornan and Usher were disputing their bill.

Despite Usher's continuing and often volatile threats to "buy the whole bloody place" the manager was still insisting that the bill be paid in full. Eventually Usher paid but Cornan didn't – well, not until the next morning when he had to return for his coat that he left behind!

The hotel bar – what bliss those three little words conjure up! It had been used quite extensively that night, but unfortunately ran out of Pernod, amongst other things, which accounted for Hambo being the first to chunder because "Dammit! I had to start drinking double brandies."

Saturday dawned, and with no game a sightseeing tour of York seemed a good idea. Unfortunately, no one got further than a little pub not a few hundred yards away from the hotel which, as if by magic, was opening its doors at 11.00 a.m. prompt as we strolled past. As you can imagine, a tremendous piss-up ensued. Even Collomosse bought a round. All the songs were sung (some twice), and numerous people were ill. John Davies got into such a muddle that when we all left he missed the bus and had to take a taxi into town. It only cost him £4 (£1 a goal) – not a bad bargain, eh, John?

Saturday night? Ah yes, Saturday night – the night we had all been waiting for. More girls than you could imagine, more booze than you could drink, more bullshit than you have ever heard – the night York will never forget! The night of the PARTY! As with most things that Roger Entwistle gets involved in, not only was it a disaster, a catastrophe even, but the bloody thing couldn't even be found! As gangs of disconsolate Old Croydonians returned to the hotel after searching the whole of York, they were met with a cheery sight in the hotel bar. The ones who knew what Roger was like had stayed behind and were all well on the way, not only with the booze but with four birds – one fat, one ugly, one spotty and one bespectacled, obviously all grateful for male company. Ours because no one else in his right mind would touch them.

Whilst not raving beauties they did serve their purpose over the next three days, keeping the lads 'entertained'; and as soon as Filbey gets the rash we'll all be down at Croydon General for the umbrella. Friendly lasses these Northerners – even in the changing rooms, eh, Tim?

On Sunday morning the number for breakfast had sadly diminished. Eyes were sore and bloodshot (together with certain other things), and during the morning's cribbage contest cards were laid very softly. (This was also due to the fact that Hambridge and Hodges had managed to demolish a large marble-topped table during a tackle contest the previous night.)

Cornan, Glassington and Blake had disappeared altogether by the time we reached Pocklington for the afternoon game. They eventually arrived slightly the worse for wear, but we still managed to trounce the locals 20–0, despite Glassington's touchline barracking.

That evening we drank the Pocklington bar dry. Entwistle stripped and, to be quite honest, the drink got the better of me and I can't remember much else. Suffice to say, it was a good one. By the time we had returned to the hotel bar for sanctuary and serious drinking, the old marbles were beginning to clear. The four lovelies from the previous night had returned and were once again being put to good use by those left out before. Dave Yeovil drunk a glass of TCP and water thinking it was Pernod and was promptly sick all over Roger, who returned the compliment immediately all over

One fat, one ugly, one spotty and one bespectacled.

him. That night was probably the best of the whole tour, which is why I can say these things. No one can remember a thing.

Monday – I got up, fed, packed and went off to York for the final game to play the local champions. It was a terrible day – cold, wet and miserable and not ideal by any stretch of the imagination to play a good game, especially with everyone feeling sick and jaded. However, we did manage some good rugby. In fact, it was quite superb at times, and only to lose 10–9 was amazing. Hats off to Gill (try) and Entwistle (conversion and penalty); what a boot!

As it was the last real opportunity to get some proper drinking done (and to have the hair of the dog) we set about our task quite well really and managed to drink York's bar dry in a short while. By seven o'clock we were all on board the 7.10 p.m. from York to London, much to the relief of everyone on the 7.15, no doubt.

Three hours later a train pulled into King's Cross to disgorge a load of holidaymakers who had enjoyed Easter up until 7.10 p.m. that night – until they met us! Most of the girls, including the ugly, fat, spotty and bespectacled, had been chatted up, molested, manhandled and assaulted. Complaints flew, but it was too late. The dishevelled, drunk and excessively tired but extremely contented Old Croydonians were home.

York will never be the same again; neither will Joan, Trudy, Anne and Marion, but that's another story!

ROGER ENTWISTLE'S MAGICAL MYSTERY TOUR

In this world there are those who possess great organising ability. There are others, however, to whom the task of running a public convenience with more than one seat poses a problem of Olympian proportions.

Then there's Roger!

The First Day:
In view of the fact that our flights had been switched from Gatwick to Heathrow, the twenty-two tour members were now obliged to make their own way to the destination by car. We had all been instructed to bring sleeping bags as the overnight arrangements had not been finalised. All this was four days before we were to depart. It should have come as no surprise when the coach that was to take us to Heathrow was also an hour late.

Nonetheless we managed to catch the right plane (with only one ticket being made out in the wrong name) and eventually found ourselves at Lyons Airport, 80° in the shade, at 5 p.m.

We were quite looking forward to the fifty-or-so-mile journey to Villeneuve D'Allier (and were no doubt as surprised as the five car drivers sent to collect twenty-two tour members and their kit that we did not fit easily into the five small cars provided. Still, what is a little discomfort for an hour or so? Did I say an hour? Roger had apparently not looked at the map, but had *assumed* it was only fifty miles. It turned out to be more like 250 miles. Thanks, Rog.

Personally, the novelty of sharing a small Citröen with four hefty lads, one of whom became the first registered chunderer of the tour – very pleasant at 80° – soon wore off. And after six hours, it was, to say the least, beginning to pall a little. Our driver – and I use the word loosely as it would appear that a full complement of limbs and a maniacal desire for some posthumous award entitles one to a licence in France – deposited us at the hotel at about 11.15 p.m. The rest of the party had already arrived and were tucking into cold salami, omelette and red wine – just the ticket when one hasn't eaten for twelve hours.

Still, we were all present and correct – but no, a car was missing! Three cars got off the ferry at Calais but only two had arrived. Missing persons: Church J., Streeter R. and the Collomosses P. and J. Apparently they had some overheating problems in Paris (the cars not the passengers). Roger, their leader, had not waited, of course. He raced ahead with the map leaving the lads hopelessly lost.

After thirty hours or so together in a car, I suppose four blokes should get to know one another quite well. They arrived at 12.30 a.m. just as the rest of us were getting to know the local red wine – an unpretentious little number, which Morley Owen described as 'red ink'. What can you expect at 30p a litre?

At around 3.00 a.m. the question of sleeping arrangements began to creep into our minds. "No sweat," said Roger (a standard reply for "Why ask me? I'm only the tour manager"), and indeed there was no sweat. There were also no beds, no hot water and no central heating in the three unfurnished houses supplied to us by the mayor for our accommodation. Roger had warned us all that anyone responsible for damage to the mayor's property would be answerable to him. Quite what he expected us to do to four bare stone walls, stone floors, foam mattresses and woolly blankets, I'm not quite sure.

Our first French night settled over the 'Olympic Village',

as Cornan christened it. Drunken mutterings and furtive comments about Roger's personal well-being echoed around the stony walls, as he was a guest of the mayor with a proper bed and working toilet.

The Second Day:
It was a beautiful morning and, as Roger had promised, an idyllic setting. The village was set on the side of a deep valley with the River Allier meandering through, and small streams tinkling down verdant hillsides. A church set high on the opposite side of the valley dominated a picturebook landscape, with vineyards, allotments, and cattle and sheep grazing lazily with the local peasants working in the fields. It was one of those places where the boot of industrial progress had not left its footprint, where time stood still, and where the rush and bustle of the modern world had passed by – a truly peaceful and tranquil setting. Can you think of a worse bloody place to bring thirty-one people on a rugby tour? I wouldn't say it was quiet, but they organised a bus once a week to go to the nearest town to watch the traffic lights change!

There were, however, three bars in the village – some slight relief.

Languejacq, our opponents for the first game, had invited us to their village for drinks before the game. I cannot describe what festivities took place, as I was one of the unfortunate four who got left behind without a lift. I gather, though, that Cornan, Glassington, Houghton and myself had a better time than our twenty-seven compatriots and didn't have to travel twenty miles each way for the privilege. Not only did Roger manage to forget us four, but also, when the party returned for lunch and their kit, he balanced things by leaving four people at Languejacq. Out of these unfortunates was Hambridge, who later took the field, just for five minutes, and was promptly stretchered off after injuring his ankle.

The match, played in Languejacq Stadium, was a pleasant affair, watched by about 300 people. We eventually ran out

Quite what he expected us to do to four bare stone walls, stone floors, foam mattresses and woolly blankets, I'm not quite sure

as winners, 14–12 after being 4–12 down.

Their clubhouse was in a cellar in the village, and a most enormous piss-up ensued. Hambo and Cornan were the two main casualties and, although both passed out around sevenish, by the time we had all assembled for the evening meal at our hotel they were at least upright. To prove he was awake, Cornan kept making speeches, but by now the tour was thirty-six hours old and his voice, mercifully, had disappeared.

We entertained the opposition in grand style with an enormous bunfight and then proceeded to visit the local disco in Brioude – the nearest town. Here we met a number of the following day's opposition and they seemed quite pleased to find that half our side couldn't even stand up. The disco did give us all a chance to try out our French by chatting up the local lovelies. Glassington tried immensely hard and, as usual, was unsuccessful. It came as no surprise that we all returned to our foam mattresses empty handed.

The Third Day:

Cornan, Houghton and Harold appeared to be the main casualties from the previous night. Harold had slept on the gravel in the hotel car park and looked like it. Houghton's idea of coffee and brandy had seemed to remove the lining from his insides quite successfully and Cornan had suffered a severe relapse after taking the hair of the dog.

After a morning of drifting from bar to bar, a splendid lunch of mixed veg with fish cream, fatty pork and greasy chips followed by cream cheese saw off those with weak constitutions, but all were assembled for the big one against Brioude.

Now, no one has ever questioned Roger's ability to bullshit. In fact, for those who don't know him it might be possible to accept some of his claims as quite passable. Quite what he said to warrant a fixture against Brioude one shudders to think. They play in the French Division Two and can therefore be compared with the likes of Blackheath, Saracens or Sale.

A stadium somewhat larger than Streatham-Croydon's and an admission of £1.25 per head gives you an idea of the standard.

A little curtain-raiser of a Languejacq/OC XV versus Brioude 2nd XV (result: 6–55) paved the way for a match against the Brioude 1st XV, in which we came off the wrong end of 49–0. Strangely enough, though, we didn't actually disgrace ourselves and could have scored two or three times were it not for fatigue due to rather too much red wine. Indeed, some twenty-seven points came in the last twenty minutes, when the revelries of the previous days took their toll. One person who came off the pitch with his reputation truly enhanced was Trevor Neckles, now known to one and all as Snowflake, whom the crowd of around 600 or so really took to their hearts with his uncompromising style of play. They were shouting, *"La neige!"* every time he had the ball.

Another massive bunfight meal took place that night, and as the hotelier could take no more he shut at 11.00 p.m. We were therefore forced to split up and visit various village discos, fairs, etc. in the outlying regions. At one particular disco our worst fears were confirmed – French blokes dancing with other French blokes. Backs to the wall lads, and home to the Olympic Village.

The Fourth Day:

Breakfast was very poorly attended. This was our last chance to visit our three bars and to have a farewell lunch. No one was particularly looking forward to another five hours in a car, so we hired a coach. Not a coach for twenty-two – oh no, that would have been too easy – but a coach for fifteen was more than adequate. We left at 11.15 a.m. to catch the 6.00 p.m. flight, but, just to add a bit of spice to the journey, the driver took us by the scenic route and we eventually arrived at 5.50 p.m. Still, the scenery was splendid.

We boarded the plane, and before we knew it we were in The Tamworth Arms supping copious pints of Young's ale. About 9.30 things started to get a bit boisterous, and when someone rather sarcastically told the landlord that we had come all the way from the south of France to visit his palatial and gloriously decorated hostelry he refused to serve us thinking we were extracting the urine. However, diplomatic relations were restored and a good time was had by all. Sorrell was heard to remark that it was the best piss-up that he'd had all tour, but what else can you expect for £70 when Roger takes command?

CIRENCESTER IN THE SPRING

Well the day had arrived again; another year had gone by. It was *that* Friday again – the Friday that all rugby players, and Dave Hambridge, wait patiently for – and this year, as all years, the Old Croydonians were on their way to wreak havoc and destruction on some poor unsuspecting town. This year it was the turn of the Cotswolds and a sleepy little town called Cirencester. Not since the Romans marched in all those years ago was it to see such a spectacle. The 'meet' was arranged at Croydon Town Hall at 9.00 a.m. Along strolled Howard Cooper at 9.20 a.m. full of apologies: "Sorry, lads. Had to take the missus a cup of tea in bed." I've never heard it called that before!

We were just about to leave when the organiser realised that our interpreter had failed to show. Someone suggested that he got the weeks messed up, or that he was waiting at Tavistock Road. It was decided to leave without him as we all thought that he'd gone to Villeneuve D'Allier to brush up on his English. Still, as it turned out, the Gnat's great gift with languages was not needed; listening to Glassington and Cornan ohh-ahh-arring all the way down gave us great confidence that we could at least communicate with the locals in some small way.

There was rather a lack of booze on the coach (oh, for the days of Usher with his suitcase of one pair of pants, a toothbrush, thirty cans of Guinness and a stack of dirty magazines!), and so by the time we stopped everyone was

Oh, for the days of Usher with his suitcase!

dying for a pint. But this was not to be – we could hardly get into the café for a cup of tea, and that was dry. It was here that we met up with our fellow travellers, Dick, Jean, John and Steve, Bec Old Boys, Old Wimbledonians and many others.

The rest of the journey passed with everyone waiting for twelve o'clock, which came and went, much to the disgust of Animal, who proceeded to give our driver a minute-by-minute countdown of every valuable minute of drinking time lost. On our arrival at the hotel, there was the usual rush to avoid sharing with Crow and Animal, who, to everyone's relief, ended up sharing with each other; the sweet music they made had to be heard to be believed. The next move, of course, was straight to the nearest pub, where vast quantities of alcohol were to be consumed – this in spite of the approaching game. Of course, the journey to the game started late and by the time our navigator, who insisted he knew where he was going, had got us on our way,we were an hour late.

We finally arrived and turned out for the game; and it is here that I must say the defeat by Brioude was rather less embarrassing than the defeat we suffered at the hands of Dursley, who had considerably less talent. Down to fourteen men we were swamped in the second half and lost by thirty points. The après game wasn't particularly exciting with our morale deflated and a lot of their players departing and most of our supporters sober. Our departure was followed by a guided tour by Bert around Gloucester, trying to find a particular pub, which we eventually came to. Our driver gave us strict instructions for leaving within an hour, which meant we drank as much beer and sang as many of the loudest songs we could – in fact, we were on the verge of being evicted when we had to leave. On arrival back at base people tended to go their own way – Parsley and Carrot after the Venison, us more serious drinkers into the nearest pub.

And so to our first night in the hotel – what a disaster! – culminating in the bar closing early. There was the famous Glassington tightrope walk across the tabletops and bar; there was Picasso Animal painting O.C.R.F.C. across every mirror and wall he could find; there was the skip sleeping soundly in the corner, and last but not least the Croydonian Anglican Choir broke into song again.

The second day broke clear and bright with the awful-looking faces at breakfast and the usual crew who never made it. The first down was Parsley, who had slept most of the previous evening anyway. Again the parties split and went to various hostelries to rid themselves of hangovers and to practise the language. It was on their return to the coach that most of the party discovered that they had no bed for the night due to the watering of mattresses whilst bodies were under deep sedation from the havoc of the previous night. The committee of elderly members sorted this out and we were allowed back under conditions.

Our journey to Old Cryptians involved Dr Boffa and Collomosse aiding a girl who had been in an accident (poor old Boff, this was to be a busman's holiday), and Mattey becoming the axeman of Cirencester. The game itself was both exciting and full of good rugby, with us going down a couple of points. It is at this stage where my memory fades rather fast. I believe Rip Van Winkle fell asleep again; Ray Streeter became our boot-drinking champion; the Pipe did 'Eskimo Nell' yet again; and I ended up in Gloucester Infirmary. It was fortunate that I didn't really miss anything. True to his word, the manager closed the bar at 11 p.m. and people retired to bed.

Sunday was again a disjointed day with the gamblers setting up an expensive card school at the hotel and others watching Kojak play rugby at Old Cryptians against a French side. This latter squad proceeded to get very pissed and very noisy and we ended up monopolising the Cryptians' bar yet again. It was during this period that the kleptomaniac struck again and the huge red letters O.C.R.F.C. disappeared from outside the clubhouse. The people who were there that afternoon left a lot of good friends behind when they departed, including a taxi driver who squeezed eight of us into his car.

The evening was probably the best of the tour with everybody together in The Fleece drinking and singing. Arriving back at the hotel, the manager again closed the bar at 12.00; some of us crept up to bed while others argued. Mattey was led from the bar serenading the manager, who had him in a half nelson. I do not think that 'Blue Moon' has sounded as good since Sinatra. The rest, tired of arguing, eventually went to bed, only to find there weren't enough beds to go around. Somehow Pollard had stolen Mattey's bed; and someone had stolen Sorrell's. We thought at this point the manager was about to crack as Mattey, still humming 'Blue Moon', pointed out to him that we didn't seem to have as many beds as we had had before. It was strange to see the change in the man. He had spent most of the evening looking over his shoulder expecting to see the Animal, with his newly acquired air rifle stalking him.

The last day arrived, and for once we all found ourselves in the same hostelry. We saw some marvellous formation dancing from Glassington and Church junior (poor Church senior was attempting to mend the coach that had broken down). There was also the Greek dancing of Carrot and Parsley stepping out to 'Zorba', finally climaxing with Parsley nutting the floor and falling asleep again.

And so to the final game with the confrontation of Granddad and Peter Beard: they both had excellent games – in fact, all the Old Croydonians played well, especially on the last day of the tour. And so to the clubhouse, where the last day's drinking was done, and from there back to The Fleece where we gave them a final finale of 'Polly, Polly'. The coach arrived and we all boarded, tired and dreading the journey home. It was only as we were due to leave that it was discovered that Church junior was nowhere to be seen. We waited but there was no sign. Suggestions were made: he was locked in the bog, chasing Yetis, in the boot, or pissed in the corner. In the end it was decided to leave and hope Phil came across Ian Sorrell, who could give him a lift home.

The journey back was quiet, Parsley (alias "Rip Van Winkle" Cornan) was sleeping again, joined by Cooper and Hambridge, and there was only Carrot to make any noise. No, wait a minute, there he was – Morley Owen trying desperately to persuade the Old Boys' Choir into singing 'Land of my Fathers'. He would start to sing, stop and mumble something like "Come on, you bastards," and would then sit down only to rise again two minutes later threatening he would give us one more chance to sing it. He finally gave in completely when someone in the know asked him how he got barred from The Royal Standard. The silence in the coach would be shattered by the sounds of a voice screaming, "You dirty bastard, Mattey," as Nick would fire off a volley of the foulest farts imaginable and roar with laughter. This amazing feat occurred at regular five-minute intervals.

And so to Croydon where tired individuals staggered from the coach and made their way home however possible – skint, ill, but contented. Another tour had finished.

EASTER TOUR IN SCOTLAND or COME BACK, ROGER – ALL IS FORGIVEN

It is difficult to convey through the medium of the pen the icy feeling of panic which grips the entrails of a tour manager when he discovers at 8.30 the night before departure that all documents relating to the tour, including the rail tickets, are securely under lock and key in an office miles from where he is sitting.

Gone is the warm glow of excitement in anticipation of days of drunken bonhomie; gone the pleasant feeling of having overcome impossible odds in getting the bloody tour organised at all. In their place is a sensation of sulphuric acid ice cubes melting in the pit of his stomach and gently oozing through the M & S 99p 'specials' (super absorbent for the man of today).

Recalling to mind a famous saying used so often by a previous tour manager – 'No sweat' – I phoned King's Cross and explained coolly and calmly my predicament. An equally cool and calm BR supervisor dealt with my problem most sympathetically – quite simple really – NO TICKETS, NO JOURNEY. After discussions, which became increasingly less cool and calm, the supervisor said he would arrange for duplicate tickets to be available at the King's Cross travel office in the morning in time for all of us to be comfortably seated on the 9.00 a.m. to Edinburgh.

Uplifted by his confidence, I retired, awoke and presented myself at the appointed hour at the relevant ticket office. "NO TICKETS, NO JOURNEY, duplicate or otherwise. The system doesn't work like that, sir."

"But – but – but – " I stammered.

"Cancel their meat pies," roared Morley helpfully to a crowd of mildly amused, if unsympathetic, onlookers.

"Call for Roger," cried Sorrell, spotting the situation at once.

Hesitantly I wrote a personal cheque for a small fortune to purchase a new set of tickets and with literally seconds to spare we boarded the train.

I was concerned to notice that some of our reserved seats were occupied. However, a diplomatic delegation of Matthews, Manley, Church and Cornan appeared to have few problems in removing the incumbents.

We arrived in Edinburgh in no time at all – well, just about time for Phil Church to drink two bottles of Scotch; and with almost ten minutes in which to make our connection to Leuchars it was understandable that the party split up to all corners of the station in order to attend to matters at one or both ends of their alimentary canal. Small wonder therefore that Phil Church and Bob Goodwin left their cases and kit on the platform in the ensuing scramble to get on the train. Hambridge, clever old fellow that he was, watched Bob struggle on board with a tray of beer and an OC kitbag, in the full knowledge that it belonged to him. Rather than inform Bob of his error straight away, he broke the news after an hour or so.

We were met at Leuchars by Waid Academy FP RFC, shuttled to our hotels in the lovely fishing village of Anstruther, and set about getting to know the locals, or, as in the case of "Bingo" Blake, to locate the nearest venue for the game of which he now proudly bears the name.

My account of the events during the ensuing four days or so are, of course, based on personal experience, clouded on occasions by an excess of hospitality, and a mixture of hearsay and rumour, which reached my ears from notoriously unreliable sources. Consequently I claim a limited element of truth in anything that follows.

Friday night was spent by the more mature (in age, that is – not necessarily mental development) in exploring the various establishments of the village, taking liquid substances and getting to know the locals, most of whom seemed to be called Jimmy. In one particular bar, run by an appalling drunkard called Wally, who drove the village bus in his spare time, there occurred what to my knowledge was the most spirited sing-song of the tour when, spurred on by the locals, some old fool (whose name temporarily escapes me) stood on a chair for an interminable period of time roaring renditions of the old family favourites 'The Alphabet Song', 'One Night in Gay Paris', 'I Love My Mother-in-Law', etc.

The party only broke up when two Scotsmen, apparently the best of friends two minutes before, proceeded to knock seven bells out of each other in the corner of the bar – time for OCs to make a discreet exit.

On returning to my hotel I was greeted by mine host with the words that every tour manager longs to hear: "They want you at the local police station." There had been a trifling event concerning a young man (much the worse for wear), a Mercedes (in which he was found sitting with the engine running) and the owner (a local villain recently acquitted on a charge of attempted murder). Henry Kissinger could have had trouble with that lot, but in the end everything worked out okay and, with apologies all round, there ended our one and only brush with authority.

By the time I returned to the hotel, the hardened few were still in the bar. Just when things were really livening up and a good session was developing, Hambridge made a particular ungentlemanly suggestion to the wife of the landlord, who promptly shut the bar and sent us to bed.

Saturday broke bright and clear. Brian Goode and Steve Murray arrived. They had missed the train altogether, and Phil Church returned from the hotel in which he'd slept to the one in which he was booked, at least sober enough to realise that his case was still in Edinburgh – which appeared to cause him considerable amusement.

Whilst those unfortunate enough to be picked for the 'sevens' that afternoon psyched themselves up, their more fortunate colleagues reacquainted themselves with friendly Wally, who mixed a series of horrendous cocktails, typified by his Moscow mule with a Swan chaser. Bingo Blake swamped all his drinks with lager to kill the taste, and Dave Matthews was drunk enough to float a ship and knock him out for twelve hours.

Meanwhile, back at the local rugby club, the OC seven of Johnstone, Blake, Goodwin, Inchead, Hodges, Glassington and Church reached the final of the tournament, eventually going down 28–18 to Madras FP.

I remember little of Saturday evening other that it lasted until five o'clock Sunday morning. I can recall Ian Sorrell informing the local loose-head, who was built like an air-raid shelter, in graphic detail what he was going to do to him during the following afternoon's scrummaging. (In the event, Streeter demolished the unfortunate chap, who up until then had been the local's pride and joy). I also remember clearly the landlord's daughter – Morag, or was it Megan? Anyway, my wife will be reading this so I'll pass swiftly on to my most vivid recollection – that of Cornan, who, having reverted to his native tongue somewhere just East of Stepney, had donned his stupid cap at a rakish angle and proceeded to get rat-legged in his own immutable, humorous style. Each time Pat came into view, the cap a little further askew, his voice was a little more cracked. He would greet us with a cheery wave, demand a large one of whatever you fancy, down it in one and wander off to pastures new. Those of us unlucky enough to get caught on a number of occasions could only watch the demolition act with aplomb.

Some of the younger element were making headway with the local girls in the village disco, although the language barrier threw up a few problems. However, actions speak louder than words and by Sunday morning Anglo-Scots relationships seemed to have got a little better in certain quarters.

As the majority of the party were playing on Sunday

afternoon, the morning seemed to pass fairly quietly; except, that is, for Cornan whose finger was still firmly on the self-destruct button, though mercifully his voice was now reduced to an inaudible croak.

A motley OC XV took the field to play Waid Academy FP 1st XV who, despite Streeter's disruptive efforts and Johnstone's obscenely athletic display, gave us a walloping by about 23–0. The fact that they considered it their best display of the season gave us a little satisfaction.

Having awakened the thirst buds we took solace in the village and, in the continuing absence of any decent beer, consumed vast quantities of Guinness, Campari, gin, whisky and assorted cocktails. As the evening developed along fairly predictable lines, it became clear that one of our number was being singled out for the 'treatment' by a young lady (both adjective and noun being open to question) who was holidaying in the area. We watched with amusement tinged with a mixture of sympathy and horror as the female in question spun a not very subtle web, attacked and ensnared her prey. Glassington did not appear to know what had hit him and as we watched him being led out "to take her for a meal" we shook our heads ruefully and drank to his misfortune.

By the early hours of Monday morning a few stalwarts were still draped around the bar, including Manley, who did not appear to sleep during the entire tour, and Rob Johnstone, who sinks a fair amount of booze for a sports student. (His storage capacity must be improved by the distance the waste has to travel before being released.)

The last day of an Easter tour is ideal for a 10.30 a.m. kick-off. We played, and drew 12–12 with a touring side from Torquay. (In fact, we would have won, but an unbelievable refereeing decision gave them a try in the last minute.)

Having said the farewells to our excellent hosts, we could look forward to a seven-and-a-half-hour train journey. Entwistle, who had been a paragon of virtue up until this

We watched with amusement tinged with a mixture of sympathy and horror as the female in question spun a not very subtle web.

point, suddenly found his true form and acutely embarrassed us all. We were partially saved, firstly by the fact that he dropped and smashed his two little bottles of wine minutes after purchasing them, and secondly that he left the party at Edinburgh announcing that he was going to fly back.

As this option had already been explored and no seats were available on any flights to Heathrow or Gatwick, we all knew that he would never make it. But old Roger never listens. Off he went. We laughed heartily as he staggered into the distance.

The fact that he was in The Fountain Head at 7.00 that night whilst the rest of us were still somewhere north of Kettering defies all understanding. His story that he came back sitting next to the pilot, masquerading as an expectant father on a mission of mercy to his pregnant wife's bedside, is so outrageous that it is probably true.

Although we rid ourselves of one problem in Roger at Edinburgh Station, we were still faced with the prospect of five and a half hours on the train, packed to overflowing, with no seats available.

I can only put it down to the fact that I have led a devoutly religious life, that somebody up there loves me, and that, with no explanation given at all, British Rail had reserved our party eighteen seats, into which we collapsed gratefully. This piece of good fortune restored my credibility as a tour manager and in some eyes elevated me to an almost godlike status. Despite that, all I can say is roll on next year, roll on Jersey, and good luck, Ian Sorrell.

DAWN RAID or HOW I SAW IT

This was to be a meticulously planned operation. Stealthily, from pick-up points all over southern Britain, from towns as far apart as Bristol and Edenbridge, they came. The advance party reached Shoreham, Sussex soon after dawn.

Innocently the Fokker emblazoned for the occasion in Jersey European Airways colours was undergoing its final check-over. One trooper, his face mistakenly blackened for the occasion, nervously devoured his fourth breakfast. It was a fine clear morning as the kite taxied toward the freshly briefed group assembled in scramble position. Its blunt nose seemed to rise up in defiance, pointing towards occupied Jersey. This was to be a day to remember, to be revered on many a winter's evening by the survivors back at their home base.

Initially the assault went according to plan, and by the time groups two and three were airborne the advance party had not only gained a tenuous toehold on the island, but had attacked and overcome fierce resistance in an enemy hotel and had set up a temporary strike command there. The defeated officers were floating upside down in the swimming pool!

Unfortunately, for the second assault group things were going dreadfully wrong. A leakage of a dangerous duty-free spirit-like substance directly over the throat of a parched infantryman was the cause of a break in radio silence and so the party met with heavy resistance on arrival. Fortunately, the heaviest fighting was around the airport buildings, and one group captured in the toilets was able to escape unscathed. The unfortunate infantryman at his court martial said he "hadn't a leg to stand on"!

Group three arrived on the island unobserved, and arrived in the new HQ in commandeered sports cars.

By now even Twizzle (Entwistle) will have realised that this was not 1941, but 1981, and the Old Croydonians were on tour again with eight guests from Edenbridge RFC – something that they lived to regret.

Later that day, a court-martialled Ray Streeter, still full of purloined gin, was seen to throw a bucket of water over Jean Glassington in despair at his team's defeat at the hands of Bognor. This defeat was partly the writer's fault as team selection with the aid of 'trainer' Pat Cornan only took place on the first Fokker flight. Either the side selected could not have been announced over the PA on the second flight or Ray Streeter was in rebellious mood.

Other appearances that day were in the shape of several non-swimming streakers, and quite a few clothed bathers. The evening mainly consisted of groups of players pub-crawling the square mile around the hotel, repeatedly running into previously banned groups in the next pub. The consequence of the game was that, collectively, we were all banned from all pubs, but splinter groups were only banned from some pubs. Where you could go all depended on whom you were with.

Day two saw Usher heavily into long-life at breakfast (an old trick of his), whilst spurning stewed prunes and the like. Your reporter joined Snowflake, Usher, and one other heavyweight (unnamed) to borrow a car from the colleague of the suntanned gentleman. The car turned out to be a Mini – not quite what Trevor had in mind. Main memories of the day were of a strange hat of basically Australian origin (a loose term), which we were never again without, and putting Manley into the boot of the Mini. This was necessary for two reasons: one, to stop him from spraying the high street and two, because the Mini was already full of heavyweights.

Later that afternoon Animal slept through another close defeat at the hands of Jersey RFC. Personally, my evening was spent trying to gain entry to Dick Glassington's swanky hotel with Steve Davies from Edenbridge and Roger the Todger.

This was eventually achieved at around 3.00 a.m., to find John Collomosse had been in there all evening. Apologies to Steve Davenport for getting him out of bed on the intercom.

Another story worth relating concerns a motley bunch consisting of Animal, Manley, Tony Leach and Martin Wilkinson. They were apparently refused entrance to one of the smarter discos on generally 'decrepit' appearance grounds. Now this must have been some confrontation, as our stalwarts weighed in at 75 stone versus 100 stones of six bouncers and the manager. The conversation went roughly: "Can't let you in, boys," said the manager. "Bollocks," said the lads and promptly walked in, which was just as well as Norman Blake was asleep in the corner.

Day three dawned. Hangover pills and hat and pyjamas at breakfast – no Usher this time. The morning passed peacefully enough for everyone except Paul Goodwin. He spotted a number of the fair sex at approximately three yards through squinted minces and glasses, and burrowed into Dixons at a fearful pace to emerge later, minus female and £90, with a Box Brownie. He was also muttering something about selling Bob the one with black cloth and squeeze bulb. Thick as thieves these Goodwins – no chance of sharing such wise investments with their clubmates! Painfully we lost to Hartlepool Rovers that afternoon, in spite of Streeter (now recovered, ribs and all) completely destroying their front row. A little expansion is required before we move on from this game. Our opposition brought sixty-five to eighty-five (mainly players) in their party, all kitted out in club jumpers and ties together with white shirts, etc. On the pitch Steve Hayward and an opponent were sent off for fighting. Steve needed five stitches, as his ear had been bitten, but (of course) hit the wrong bloke, who went off as well.

Snowflake and Usher really came into their own now in the borrowed Mini. With the speed of light and laser-beam accuracy they whisked Steve to the hospital. Unfortunately for Steve, whilst his stitches were being inserted, Usher found a pub with the 'best part of the barrel' currently on distribution, and Trevor was convinced that the 25p nips that he was receiving were not in fact Safeway's, as the bottle suggested, but twelve-year-old Chivas Regal. (John Lynch has apparently gone into the drinks export market.)

This left Steve in a sticky situation. Bleeding and in rugby kit he had been banned from the pub and was walking back to the ground several miles away. Most people thought it was a charity walk and he raised enough for a pint of crème de menthe for his troubles. Exit Usher and Snowflake.

That night we returned to the rugby club by coach and a veritable drinking orgy ensued, most of which can remain unremembered. One or two notable happenings concerned Steve Hayward (again). Was he still in his rugby kit? By now Steve had really taken to the pints of 'antifreeze' frappé. Now, I've seen some cocktail waiters in action, but the way Steve emptied two ice buckets into a bar towel on the top of the counter and swung the last round his head with the agility of a hammer thrower was wonderful to behold. Unfortunately the blow he smote at this manoeuvre's conclusion almost split the bar top, and succeeded in jogging Streeter's elbow in a manor which liberally distributed Ray's pint of 'antifreeze' straight down the face of a guy conservatively sized at six eight. Undaunted, Ray scraped his glass up the giant's beard and retrieved most of the liquor. I think that the throwaway line was "You don't mind if I have my drink back now, do you?"

Later that evening your scribe needed the services of two sleuths closely resembling Sid Vicious and Johnny Rotten to get him back to the hotel. A black mark was given to the hotel manager for arranging five Black Maria's and an 'in-pokey' weekend for Sid and Johnny for their trouble.

Incidentally, Steve Davies described Sid's haircut as being put on with a T-square.

Day four was a free day and it was decided by majority (thirty-five against one) to go motor racing. Norman Blake really scored points here, looking just the part in a see-through short-sleeved shirt. Unfortunately it was blowing a force-nine gale at the time and raining stair rods!

Later that night Pat Cornan was moved to take your Levin-like reporter back to his lunchtime drinking haunt. The conversation was short and went something like: "Sorry, lads, the bar's closed." "But I spent fifty quid in here this lunchtime," complained Pat. (I'm sure that was an exaggeration). "That's right," – pause – "we've closed. On yer bike," and, despite Pat's Robin Day-like quizzing, that was it.

Later that evening the Edenbridge lads really came into their own, ably led by Ross and Terry Daikin. Their rendition of 'Nelly in the Barn', complete with bar stools pounding the ceiling, could have had the bar closed in thirty seconds flat, except that Usher's neck was across the bar top like that of an old-time Parisian aristocrat under the guillotine. Fortunately, these goings-on didn't deter Groombridge from biting everyone's ass, Cornan from falling asleep standing up with his head on a shelf, and Entwistle from descending the stairs on his hands and knees, and promptly puking up under the chairs in the bar.

The next day group one retreated at 8.00 a.m., group two at noon, and group three at midnight. Group two's plan was amended from a perfectly good Fokker with a take-off speed and distance of sixty-five knots and 200 yards (on grass), to a Trislander, the noise of which is indescribable.

That was the end of a tour which I am either trying to remember or forget – I don't know which! The prize for the nuisance of the tour goes to – Salisbury.

THE FRENCH CONNECTION III
or THE BATTLE OF ST BRIECQ

People believe that a rugby tour is enjoyable, but on the morning of March 31st, when the 154 bus was transporting me to The Royal Standard, my stomach was complaining at the thought of the four days ahead. I had been summoned into Croydon by a young boy named Waywood, who confessed that he hadn't slept all night in excitement and needed to get on the thrash. He was already wrapped around his second pint when I arrived.

Earlier in the day I had contacted the old man of the tour, Hambridge, who informed me that he wasn't going to have the whole damn rabble back at The Hambridge Arms drinking his Chateau Rothschild; and certain tour members, like Salisbury and Burnett, were banned anyway.

It was with some surprise, therefore, that at 5.30, the appointed hour, The Hambridge Arms was packed with such tourers as Snowflake Belafonte, Bing Usher, Yosser "Give Us a Job" Cameron, the Exocet twins, Glassington and the Pipe (who, when asked where his bag with a change of clothes was, replied, "Don't be silly, boy, it's only four days.").

I personally believe that if the touring party had been granted their wishes, we would have had a four-day drinking tour of Sutton, but, despite protestations from Bovingden, Blake and Usher and numerous pee stops, we arrived at the Portsmouth ferry terminal. At the terminal we picked up our two guest tourers, ex-OC Colin Penrose and "I Can Stand on My Head and Drink" Dave.

The boat trip, I am afraid, is one big blur of Calvados, of being thrown out of the restaurant, of Yosser looking green, of OCs being chased in and out of cabins that they weren't entitled to, of the Wallers trying to speak French in the disco and finally of sleeping in the spare cabin, even if it was with Snowflake and Bernie.

The morning loomed bright and clear with even the odd smattering of intelligent conversation, like "Look at that cormorant washing his donker in the sea while he's flying" and "While I was peeing out of the porthole last night, someone peed back."

The coach trip to St Briecq proved uneventful, with most people getting some extra shut-eye. On arriving at our hotel we were informed that our beds were not ready and we should have a drink and return in an hour or two. Well, that statement was like a red rag to a bull: twenty-five OCs piled into the bar opposite (by now it was 9.30 a.m.) and a whip-round was collected.

"Madame, er, *quinze* pints of beer pression, *s'il vous plais*."

"*Pardon?*"

"Er fifteen pints of that stuff."

"*Oh, non, non, non.*"

It was then with great relief that I realised she had understood me and fifteen bottles of beer appeared from the fridge to a chorus of "Wuzza! Wuzza! Wuzza!"

It was in the second bar that I was awoken by Usher, Burnett, Salisbury and Terry on their way back to the hotel for drinks. "Come on, Rog, we've got a car outside." Gratefully I slumped into the seat, only to be told that they had stolen the car from the local garage forecourt. The rest of the night, until the early hours, was spent singing along with Ian Harris while the club taxi service roamed the town picking up the strays.

The day of our match against St Briecq arrived, with everybody, including players, drinking at the bar (Snowy had consumed six large vodka and tonics by 11.00 a.m.). The match itself was hard and, at times, niggly. Unfortunately without any recognised second rows (Tony Leach retired injured after ten minutes) we were under enormous pressure in the scrums and line-outs, resulting in a serious shortage of good balls with which our backs could play.

The evening that followed proved to be another great success. A general drink and club games against our oppo was followed by grub and more drink. This time the non-playing members of the party were a little worse for wear. The Pipe, who was legless, fell over three times, dropped his box of matches on the floor and proceeded to pick them up one by one (thinking it was two at a time). He disappeared and was later found in bed (fully dressed as usual) with two black eyes and various cuts and grazes. When asked what had happened he explained that he had found a bar, which was closed, but people were inside drinking, and so he demolished the door. Well, imagine some foreign stranger breaking down the door of *your* local while you were having afters. Two other groups of the lads went discoing. Snowflake ousted three locals from a disco seat so he could sit down, and promptly fell to sleep, Steve Waywood picked up six women, but never got anywhere; and Andy Salisbury managed to attract a couple of blokes. Later on that morning our first mementos were gathered and this resulted in the arrest of Yosser and Salisbury. They both speak great French, but to everyone's surprise were given a lift home when it was known where they were from.

Sunday was brought to a close with Shaun Waller scaling the heights of the local garage roof to purloin our trophy, which was the town flag.

Two weeks later I eventually started feeling better and discovered I had left my soiled underwear in the hotel. Oh well, somewhere in St Briecq there is something that is for ever England – and the famous two pennants that Bill Crow left on the driver's bed – or so 'tis said!

SOUTHERN IRELAND, THE GUINNESS HEAVEN

Ireland is a land of fields and farmers and small towns – the land of Joyce, Yeats, O'Casey, Swift, Wilde, Geldorf and Behan. It is also a land of pubs and bars, Guinness and neat whiskey. It is probably for the latter reason that Eddie Chamberlain and Paul "Taff" Smith organised the 1996 Easter Tour to the Emerald Isle – this, and the fact that Eddie would have the chance to play against his old RFC, Fermoy.

The journey was by luxury coach, with all the facilities of a modern transatlantic aeroplane. Our departure point was beside East Croydon Station with its conveniently placed Porter and Sorter pub. Those tour members who did not arrive DOA (drunk on arrival) had their chance to open the scoring.

Despite the luxury of the coach, by the time it had crossed the Thames on the great trek north, the loo was full and overflowing. The continual pissing in the rear side door well caused a large lump of 'blue ice' falling off near Olympia.

With the destination Holyhead we drove onto the M1. Now the serious drinking (left hand) could begin – followed by some serious vomiting too. Anyone found not drinking with the correct hand or not having a copy of the tour programme was fined £1.

The nice people at Stena Sealink had very kindly, that morning, changed the crossing times to Dublin. With this in mind, it was full steam ahead, only for us to miss our ferry by a few minutes. There now followed some clever and persuasive negotiation by Taff with members of Stena's staff. (In some circles this may be construed as threatening behaviour or blackmail.) The upshot was that we were allowed to board the freight ferry rather than wait six hours until the next crossing. (Three rousing cheers for Taff!)

What a night! Tourists were seen being tossed from one side of the ship to the other. Rough seas? High winds? No, the sea was calm. There was nothing else for it: head down, arse up, right-hand drinking. *Nessun dorma,* or none shall sleep, was the order of the day. More beer, more bbeerr, moorre beeeer . . .

"Right-hand drinking. Where's your programme?"

It was now 4 a.m. and we were only 150 miles from Mitchelstown and our hotel. With our driver remarking that all the roads had been moved since he was last in Ireland, we eventually found our way from Dublin and the open road.

That famous line in Brooke's poem: "There's some corner of a foreign field that is for ever England" probably did not refer to the occasion when our driver, at speed, mechanically opened the stopcock on the chemical loo. This incident was recorded in a local paper under the headline 'Big Pile-up on the M11 – Mystery Chemical Spillage'.

The Firgrove Hotel, just on the outskirts of Mitchelstown, was every bit as good as it looked in the brochure, with obliging hosts who immediately opened the bar and kept it open until five o'clock the next morning. As it was a Bank Holiday, all the pubs and bars were closed. We were confined to barracks, "two-handed drinking" with the only distractions of the TV, a pool competition, a game of shave the eyebrows off the prop (Tim) and hunt the missing bed (Ginger). This, incidentally, disappeared immediately on our arrival, and then appeared back in his room after breakfast, only to go missing again in time for lights-out. Ginger apparently slept on the loo in his room for four nights, as he could be certain that this was the only place in the hotel room that his room-mate was sure not to piss upon. We also played shave Bob Goodwin's head – a game most players would enjoy on a weekly basis perhaps?

The 'pissing in the bar' tournament and trophy was won by Bingo, whilst the 'staggering, swaying and collapsing' shield was won hands down by Ginger, who later also won the 'lying on the floor and vomiting a 3-D map of India' silver salver. His performance during these events may have been enhanced by the cruel application to his strawberry blond locks of Nice and Easy natural light ash-brown hair colour!

The junior members of the tour included Billy Coughlan, Stuart Sorrell and Andy Howatt. These young impressionable lads were treated to songs and stories from the 'old and bold' members of the club, some of whom played in the two matches having confessed to not playing since their last tour and not cleaning their boots either!

Saturday was the day of the first game. Our drivers banned drinking on the coach – an understandable decision, as it was they who were left to clean up the piles before. After a short and enjoyable ride through what we now know to be typical beautiful Irish countryside, we arrived at Mitchelstown. Andy Salisbury immediately recced the clubhouse for trophies to steal for our own hallowed halls. A stuffed grizzly bear was discovered in the storeroom, but how would we get it through customs? The answer was simple: put a Croydonian shirt on it and pass it off as a second-row player.

With the ground as hard as concrete, and hot, stifling overcast weather, we played a much younger side who, unfortunately for us, insisted on uncontested scrums. The referee, whilst qualified, was only conversant with Gaelic-football rules and it was not until we were showered, fed and being watered that we were able to calculate that the result had been a draw.

From the clubroom we then decanted into town and Joe's Bar. "Left-hand drinking. Where's your programme?" Now the truth of our scrimmaging could be put to the test! Clanwilliam were beaten hands down. After this it was pour Dave Hambridge into the coach, and back to the hotel, open the bar. "Left-hand drinking."

The answer was simple: put a Croydonian shirt on it and pass it off as a second-row player.

That evening, the battle-hardened warriors were set loose upon the gentlefolk of Mitchelstown. Each of us have a different story to tell of that evening's events, but everyone was agreed on one thing: this was a great place and the natives a great bunch of people.

Hide Ginger's bed, "Left-hand drinking," and we were off again on the coach to Fermoy – a new club whose bar-less clubhouse made the Black Hole of Calcutta look like Claridge's. Fermoy's players probably thought we were going to be a pushover, especially when they saw the colourless face of Stuart Sorrell, our scrum half. He needed to sit quietly for half an hour on the touchline before the game. Phil Church, our veteran No. 8, was also seen by some of the Fermoy team to stagger. It was explained to them that this was not due to his advanced years but his pre-match tonic of ten large Jameson's.

Croydon played well and, although a little lacking on the wings, managed a good performance. "Right-hand drinking." After the game at Mother Reilly's Bar in town, we were all treated to the full repertoire of old boy Ken Bovington's songs. Unfortunately he could only remember the first verse of most of them.

On leaving our hotel we were informed there were no additional charges for damage, which is probably a club record. The full-sized Guide Dogs for the Blind moneybox, which had been our mascot for the two games and which was voted man of the match for the second game, reappeared in the lobby. The smiles of the hotel's staff widened as they realised our imminent departure.

On the return ferry we shared the bar with, amongst others, two returning football clubs. They began to shout as Bingo mounted the platform to sing but their jeers turned to cheers when the dulcet tones of Elvis Patel were heard. "Right-hand drinking and £1 for not having a tour programme. Who knows another song?" With land in sight and the slowing of the ship's engines, Salisbury's rendition of 'Farmer Abraham' had us all pinned down in the bar whilst most passengers were heading for their cars and the exits.

The long road back to London on our 'dry ship' was a quiet affair. Most tourists slept. They had forged friendships with players old and new in a bond which makes it an honour to be part of the game of rugby and Croydon RFC's team spirit.

TWIZZLE'S EPISTLE, ISLE OF MAN

The church bells woke me, signalling another Easter – another four days of becoming a complete wreck. I proceeded to pack, which was not at all difficult. I have never believed in too many clothes on our Easter Tour, as it just means more to carry. Anyway, with all the beer in the bag there was not too much room left. Here I was on my way to another rugby tour, another glorious piss-up. No wonder the adrenaline was flowing.

As we drove to the club, my ever patient wife turned and asked rather pleadingly, "Darling, please can we have a family Easter next year? The girls do get two weeks off and it's so disappointing when they don't see you, and you are too ill for the rest of their holidays."

"Yes darling," I promised, knowing there were 365 days before the next time.

As we pulled up to the club I heard the raucous laughter and the gurgling of beer and it was only 8 a.m.

"Don't get too drunk, dear," the wife pleaded.

"No, Daddy, don't get drunk," the children endorsed.

"Of course not," I lied, knowing full well that the next couple of days would become another haze.

"Hey, look, it's Twizzle!" The echo went round the club as I commandeered my first pint and gazed at the happy faces that I was to share my haze with, some of them already five or six pints to the good. This was the life, and these were the thirty guys that I would be living the next few days with.

The coach arrived with the driver looking extremely apprehensive as we carted twenty crates of alcoholic liquid on board and laid the first drunk of the day across the back seats. "Lads – em, you are not allowed to drink on the coach, you know," the driver said, more in hope than as an order.

"Oh, fuck off – drive. It's only a little libation," was the reply, at which he fell silent and started the engine.

The rest of the journey was a mixture of filthy songs, drinking, joking, reading dirty magazines and peeing. By the time we got to Liverpool, our destination for the ferry to the Isle of Man, the coach was a mess of empty bottles and beer cans and the driver was a physical wreck. "Enjoy yourselves, boys. Someone will fetch you when you get back. Thank God it won't be me."

Then there was the ferry in all it's glory with, at this point, happy holidaymakers filing on board. My eyes were averted to the back of the boat where in all his glory sat Blade on the container jib slowly being moved over the open sea by the Tombs turning the jib wheel. 'Oh no,' I thought as the inevitable happened and Blade started to piss into the Irish Sea. Suddenly all hell was let loose with coastguards and attendants rushing up the gangplank as though on wings but not as fast as Blade, who had mysteriously disappeared.

"Where the hell is that idiot?" shouted the man in charge. "He is not sailing on this ship."

How times had changed! The drunken body on the jib would once have been *me*! Now here I was trying to use all my powers of persuasion to placate the whole of the ship's crew – which was no easy task. "Oh, come on, Skip, it was only high spirits," I heard myself saying. "No harm was meant."

"But you did see him urinate onto the quay," he retorted.

"But he was scared" I said "and just couldn't help it. After all, he was over the sea and probably can't swim." I was amazed at how easy I found these words flowing from my lips, and how easy it was to placate a furious captain. How one changes when one gets older!

At last we were on our way, a happy, singing, drinking mob, with all to look forward to at the end of another session.

It is quite a disaster to some people, being on a boat when the weather is rough. Some were hanging over the side; some were laid out flat on the lounge floor; some were ensconced in the toilet, not knowing whether to sit or kneel; and then there was Yosser – he who might as well have been dead.

One of our more enterprising players even tried to make a little loot by selling the sick bags, but it was when he offered them to a group of nuns that it rather fell by the wayside.

At last we were there. The hotel was sought, and fun and games at choosing partners ensued. "I ain't sleeping in the same room as him, he snores like a foghorn," or "I'm not sleeping anywhere near that traffer (farter)," or "I need a quiet room to do some serious winkling."

Being a senior statesman, I paid for my own single room as my days for sharing were past. Once we were settled in, the local pubs had to be explored. I must say, there were plenty – a good thing, considering the number we were barred from. It's funny that on tour we tended to spilt up into groups until very late in the evening. Then some magnetic attraction seemed to draw everybody to the same dive. This was no exception.

A small group of elderly statesmen decided to explore the pub opposite, only to find that youngsters had already got the club barred. This did not prove too much of a handicap to us oldies with money to spend. The landlord's wife eventually succumbed to our charms, which proved to be a great mistake. The lady in question went to do some shopping, only to return to a terrible shock. We were all sat on bar stools with the bar top in line with our chests; it was then that the Donegal Donkey suggested that we drop our kecks, which we duly did, knowing full well that the barman couldn't see any change. The scream that swept round the bar when the landlady returned could be heard 100 yards away. The poor woman went hysterical when we all stood up to see what the problem was and faced her in all our

One of our more enterprising players even tried to make a little loot by selling the sick bags, but it was when he offered them to a group of nuns that it rather fell by the wayside.

manhood. Needless to say, we did not grace that bar with our company again. The evening was finished off with the usual karaoke in the roughest dive (by roughest, I mean the one with the most females) and everyone creeping home to bed exhausted. Not exactly everyone – there were the ones who had given their bodies to the local ladies.

Breakfast was a different affair. I arrived to hoots of laughter and subsequently discovered that one eyebrow, half my beard and half my moustache had disappeared, courtesy of a fanatical doctor in the squad. Other hapless beings emerged looking like Mekons from *Dr Who* or something similar, all victims of the phantom Sweeny, all swearing for revenge by the end of the tour. The only thing I could do was shave the lot off and hope I had one eyebrow left by the end of the tour. The one good thing about being my age and going on tour is the fact that I do not have to play, so I can enjoy the pre-match drinks much more than when I knew that I would be out there in the afternoon.

It was a wonderful thing, finding a small boozer on the banks of the river and drinking in the sunshine before moving closer to the pitch. The only problem was that I ended up far more pissed than any of the guys that were playing.

After watching the game, in which our guys inevitably let in a few stupid scores early on due to their inebriated state and then came from behind to score a deserved victory, the usual frivolities and rugby songs, the shedding of clothes and the inevitable rendering of 'Eskimo Nell' ensued. This was followed by that wonderful rugby thing, the beer race, which always results in more being spilt than drunk. Then we went back to town to imbibe more beer; and then to the curry house, where the usual sport of throwing more than you ate was enjoyed by all. Eventually two of the lads did a runner, and an argument about whether they were with us or not and whether we should pay anyway resulted in the usual ejection and ban.

It was the following morning when it was noticed that certain members were missing again. Investigations ensued as to the suitability of their companions from the night before. This was always a wonderful talking point: the size of her, the availability, has she a friend, etc. For the next couple of days, guys would be inspecting their todgers to see if any strange creatures had invaded the nether regions. The numbers that actually end up with problems are few, but they are never allowed to forget it.

The tour from here took on a similar pattern to the first day with copious pints of ale being drunk, another win from the players and the usual divesting of clothes. A few special points spring to mind: a naked swim in the ice-cold Irish Sea, leading to the loss of one's only underpants, which proved rather uncomfortable the following day; the drinking dry of the two local pubs we were still allowed into; the last curry, which I remember nothing about and found in my bed; and the Sweeny Todd's doctor's shoes, which someone had dumped into and shoved a dead rat into one and a dead pigeon into the other.

Then we returned home. Being an oldie, I flew, and I made my local by midday just to finish off another Easter.

CROYDONIANS TOUR THE WEST COUNTRY

It was 8.00 a.m. on Good Friday, 1993. The place was East Croydon. The tour party began to arrive, many suffering from the effects of eve-of-tour drinking sessions. For some it was a familiar scene; for a few virgin tourists nervous anticipation was apparent.

The arrival of Andy Salisbury, who is a seasoned tourist (a fact which is all too evident from his sagging gut and wrinkled expression), brought smiles to the faces of the assembled throng. He leapt from a car laden with beer and lager to keep all refreshed on the journey to Gloucester.

It was the Adonis-like Ray Sutherland who got the tour off with a bang – or rather a haircut. The Stuart Barnes of CRFC had shaven his head especially for the tour – a stunt that was copied later that weekend by Taff Smith and Martin Gray, the youthful tour manager Tony Pollard and the ageing captain Mark "Northern Git" Gartland.

We set off and, having only travelled a short while, we were faced by the awesome sight of John Davies out on his morning run. However, when he was passed by a ninety-two-year-old pensioner with a Zimmer frame we realised it was just as well that he wasn't on the tour. (Editor's note: it was fortunate you saw me at the start of my run; you wouldn't have been so impressed an hour later!)

Sometime later we arrived in Nailsworth. The Egypt Mill Hotel was to be home for most of this happy crew for the next three nights. They were the lucky ones. Some of the others of the group were to enjoy the delights of two rather seedy bed-and-breakfast houses. One was run by the local frustrated divorcee, so we left Cheetham and Usher to keep her satisfied. The other, being only marginally more luxurious than the Seaman's Mission, was to be suffered by the manager and the captain. However, the Five Days guest house did witness the momentous occasion of one of our lads becoming a man with a lovely girl so pure and sweet (poetic licence in the extreme).

The appearance of Vince Dunne the following day ensured that things were going to become eventful, to say the least, and they did.

That morning we set off for Minchinhampton for our first game. The excesses of the previous night resulted in Croydon conceding twelve points in as many minutes. However, a second-half rally, including stunning tries by Dodo and Austin, resulted in an enjoyable game littered with basic errors – typical tour rugby, final score 24–36 to Minchinhampton.

That night heralded a new star in the guise of Les Clark. His attempted swim in the Egypt Mill stream resulted in several stitches in a head wound and a night in hospital, despite the efforts of John Collomosse in trying to keep him from medical aid. Thankfully John's diagnosis was slightly off the mark for once.

Sunday's match was against Gloucester Prison Service. Our lads did not welcome an early kick-off, but, unphased by minor problems, we played much better than the day before, with notable performances by Vince Dunne, Alan Doe and Mark Dodd. It was a closely fought affair, where a fair result would have been a draw, but it was marred by an extremely fortuitous score under the posts easily converted. The result was a 0–7 defeat for OCRFC. The officers' post-match hospitality was enjoyed by all.

The early part of Sunday was spent visiting a few local pubs and sampling the delights of the local Indian restaurant. The latter part of the evening was taken up by the Egypt Mill disco. This was a most interesting event, where any half-decent girl in Nailsworth stayed at home giving all the local dogs a chance of scoring – or so it seemed. This could, however, be explained away by the fact that any girl of average intelligence and looks could not possibly be impressed by the stumbling, inadequate chat-up tactics of a bunch of drunken rugby players.

Our final day had been planned to precision months in advance by Roger "I Know Everyone Who's Ever Played International Rugby" Entwistle. With bags packed and loaded on the coach, we stopped at The Halfway House for a few drinks and then on to another pub, of which I cannot recall the name, for a few more, and then to another, which I've also forgotten, for more beer and a barbecue.

Roger's planning and timing are renowned the world over. The commencement of the barbecue coincided with the worst weather conditions seen in Gloucestershire since the great flood. This did not, however, spoil the fun. That is unless you happen to be the captain of a rugby team on the last day of a tour, who after having his shirt torn from his back spent the next hour handcuffed, with his jeans and boxer shorts round his ankles and a pint jug tied to his manhood. The only way he could enjoy the drinks that were freely available was with the assistance of the locals.

Finally, completely drunk, we returned to Croydon, where some people, who really didn't know when the party was over, called into The Oval to carry on drinking and abusing their livers.

I cannot finish without one or two special mentions. Firstly, John Blake managed to turn up on tour with no money at all. Why? I hear you ask. The answer: John decided to have a drink the night before tour and, being a cautious fellow, hid his money at home for safe keeping – so safe, in fact, that next morning he had forgotten where he had hidden it.

Who will ever forget Martin Gray's impression of the Doe Brothers, the singing ability of Vince Dunne, the drinking ability of Andy Salisbury or the sight of Cheetham and Usher's clothes adorning the trees and bushes around Egypt Mill? Those clothes went missing on the first day and weren't returned till the last, when they turned up on an island.

EASTER TOUR TO EXETER

This is a brief summary of the more notable events to occur on this tour. Owing to the rigorous training regime, and relentless itinerary of matches, the accuracy of this report may be subject to considerable interpretation.

Friday 14th April:

We departed by coach from East Croydon. Everyone turned up on time, there was plenty of beer and a liberally minded coach driver – so far so good.

Our first stop was at a small pub just outside Reading. Most tour party members were wearing their 12" bow ties; those who were not were fined. Approximately ninety minutes later everyone was counted back onto the coach. First hiccup: Andy had made a friend and wanted to bring him on tour. No problem, I wouldn't have to share a room with Andy!

This person had no beer, no money and, worse still, couldn't play rugby. However, the coach left and in a few short hours we were approaching the outskirts of Exeter. Sitting at the front of the coach I heard a familiar ring of, "Pack it in, we're all mates," followed by a crunching noise as the reclining mechanism of one of the coach's seats broke.

It appeared that Andy's friend had threatened to break some legs – not just any legs, but Ginger Dunne's! So, bleeding a little, with no money and a huge black eye, this misguided soul was left on the outskirts of Exeter at least 150 miles from where we picked him up. Oh, shit! Who was going to share with Andy?

We soon arrived at the Bystock Hotel in Exeter. Building work was being carried out on the ground floor, there was a tatty carpet and curtains, and a dingy little bar in the basement – a real home from home. The most memorable part of Friday evening was Paul Langley's attempt to find someone to "teach him how to fight" – yes, Surrey Constabulary's answer to Dixon of Dock Green felt that he must learn how to fight.

Remarkably, after a day of drinking, Paul could find no takers. Also on this the first night of the tour Roger Entwistle played pool naked, Bingo sang Elvis songs and Taff began to wind up Jon Milne. So, you see, everyone felt completely at home.

Saturday 15th April:
Breakfast was at 8.30 a.m. The talk of the tables consisted of the important aspects of our strategy and tactics. You could cut the air with a knife. The tension was rising, the anticipation was almost overwhelming. It was at this point I had to remind everyone that we had to play rugby. (Always one boring git on tour, eh?)

People relaxed in their own ways throughout the morning, so much so that by kick-off at least thirteen players were as relaxed as newts. The game began. It was a hot day, there was a dry pitch, and there were lots of spectators. Five minutes into the game, there was a scrummage near their line, a back-row move, the drive into the maul and Jon Milne went over for our first try. It was 5–0 and the tourists were looking good. The details of the rest of the game are a little cloudy. I know we all drank neat vodka at half time and some more tries were scored, but, despite this being a largely up-and-back affair, Crediton RFC managed to steal victory from the clutches of defeat by a mere 105 points in the last seventy-five minutes of the game.

And so to the bar, where there was plenty of singing and an exchange of gifts. Chris Blake won the 'bottle-walking'

Also on this the first night of the tour Roger Entwistle played pool naked.

competition; Andy won the 'sing the first line of a song and then give up' competition; and I won the 'who can drink a bottle of vodka?' competition. Yes, it is beyond this point that my addled brain cannot remember any more.

A few of the stories you may like to pursue are: How did Mike Pendleton fall asleep on a bottletop and pick up a bill for £100? or How does Ginge make a name for himself again? or Where does Tim Elmes put all that beer?

Sunday 16th April:

Breakfast was at 8.30 a.m. I arrived shamefaced after being put to bed at 9.30 p.m. the previous evening not to be seen again. The usual banter ensued. This morning most party members decide to relax on the luxurious terrace (beer garden). Richard Cameron thought of a good game of throwing carrier bags full of water out of the window onto unsuspecting people below.

At 2 p.m. we left the hotel for Exeter Saracens. We took the field as fifteen of the saddest cripples, misfits and low life that you have ever seen. If we were relaxed on Saturday, we were positively catatonic by this time. Five minutes into the game and it's that man Milne again – 5–0 to us. We were all determined that yesterday's performance was not to be repeated. The final score was something in the region of 35–5. We had lost again but, considering that our backs couldn't run and our forwards couldn't push, it wasn't too bad.

And so to the bar, where a very light-hearted evening followed. There were a number of court hearings for minor misdemeanours, and Ken Bovingden crawled around the bowling green without clothes howling like a dog. I'm not sure whether this was his sentence, I just remember him doing it. Roger Entwistle begged to be ordered to remove his clothes, so as punishment he was only allowed to remove his shoes.

We returned for the last time to our hotel, where we had some more beer, and then went into town, where a 'group of us found a cider house selling the stuff for only £1 per pint.

There is a God! We enjoyed a final good sing-song and then returned to the hotel, where an elite group of drinkers and myself drank into the early hours. A few mysteries were pondered in these last few hours: Who was that strange woman? Who was that strange woman's daughter? How come Taff is still alive? Where's Mike Pendleton? And what is that strange smell?

Monday 17th April:
It was the last day, and we were going home. Now I knew how the marines felt in Vietnam. Our tour of duty was over. We all packed our bags, returned our keys and returned to the bar for the last two or three pints. Now, as you may have guessed, Mike Pendleton had left on important business or something. Next to leave was Roger Entwistle mumbling something about shoes, and that someone had dumped in one and left a dead rat in the other – and he said he'd be in the pub by 12.30. Oh well, more room on the coach for the rest of us. Shortly afterwards Jon Milne approached, dishevelled and worn out, mumbling something about Welsh gits – "Paul and I are getting the train home. See you next season." I was beginning to think that I would be the only person to be travelling home by coach. Surely no one else would drop out. Oh yes, Simon Mayall was staying down to spend some time with his parents.

The journey home was fairly subdued. A more nervous driver allowed us to stop for only an hour – wise move that!

EASTER TOUR TO STROUD

The long weekend was marred only by the actions of the hotel receptionist in the guise of Mrs Taylor. This female Basil Fawlty made Genghis Khan look like one of the Spice Girls in comparison. Admittedly, drunken behaviour caused damage to two hotel room doors and this is unfortunate and regrettable, but the appalling (and I assume sober) way in which Mrs T dealt with the situation astounded yours truly. Mrs T's reaction was to close the bar by barricading its doors with large pot plants and demanding £550 for the repair of the 'solid oak' doors, which were in fact chipboard. A figure of £300 was eventually agreed after Taffy Smith brought in an outside builder to quote. The final negotiation delayed our departure by two hours and wasted valuable drinking time. At this point some of the more seasoned members of our party were close to collapse with dehydration and lack of blood in their alcohol stream. I suggest the proprietors of that establishment stick a broom up Mrs T's arse, so at least she can do some good sweeping up as she walks around the hotel. We should all get down on our knees and thank God we are not married to her.

Did you hear the joke about the rugby club tourists who didn't get drunk and didn't cause any damage on the tour? The teams? Mother Teresa of Calcutta XV (18 points) and Hare Krishna Old Boys (24 points).

When booking next year's accommodation we should perhaps declare ourselves as a touring rugby club rather that a sporting club, or if we continue to use this euphemism we should turn up at reception each carrying hockey sticks or lacrosse rackets. Perhaps it's time to think about wearing blazers and ties to appear more respectable. In this way, when Taffy Smith whips out his todger in the bar and stirs his beer, viewing members of the public are sure not to take offence against a well-dressed sporting gentleman.

But enough of the sour grapes and on with the tour proper: The three-hour journey to Berkeley outside Stroud was punctuated by a very welcome stop at a public house. The landlord had been telephoned in advance by Eddie, our driver. This was all in all a dizzy affair, which had nothing at all to do with the 200 cans of beer already consumed, but more to do with the disorientation felt when having to wear one of Taffy Smith's eye patches. If the £1 fines from the usual left-hand, right-hand, both-hands drinking wasn't enough, we now had to cope with knowing over which eye we should wear our patch – although it did have its uses.

After copious amounts of booze it could be worn in order to cut out any double vision that one may have experienced. Perhaps that is why Long John Silver was known to wear one. And he was always legless – "Ah har, dirty parrot, he's shit on me shoulder. Pieces of nine." (It was eight, but Taffy fined him a pound for having such a stupid hat.)

Attempts to remove a Victorian copper warming pan were thwarted when the landlord's mother saw it sailing across the car park. Despite my offer of £60 it remains rawl-bolted and alarmed on the wall.

After settling in at the hotel we were taxied to Dursley, our local village, where more beer (left- and right-hand varieties) was consumed along with plates of curry. We drank nightcaps in the hotel before it was up the stairs to Bedfordshire. Little did we sleeping tourists know that Gandhi was working his wicked revenge. If it wasn't for the team tube of preparation H (although I prefer the Anusol industrial strength myself), It may not have been possible to play rugby the next day. Mark Pollard and Andy Daly were especially blighted. Stepping very slowly from the coach they looked tense and pale as if they had accidentally dropped the soap in the shower after a Larry Grayson/Quentin Crisp XV benefit match.

A little ditty springs to mind here, it goes thus (sung to the tune of 'Chim Chim Cheree'):

Ring-stinga-me ring-stinga-me ring-sting-ta-ree
Look out on the pitch when we have a curry;
Ring-stinga-me ring-stinga-me ring-sting-aroo
We'd rather have clap than a hot vindaloo.

Ring-stinga-me ring-stinga-me ring-sting-ta-ree
Pollard's piles are blocked with an onion bhaji;
Ring-stinga-me ring-stinga-me ring-sting-aroo
Daly's bum's stuck to the pan in the loo.

Another pirate who played a prominent part in the tour was Roger "Grey Beard" Entwistle who, despite having a long association with Minchinhampton (our first-game opponents) and, being an ex-Croydonian, was spared no quarter as every time he rose to speak the rest of the crew began to hum the theme tune from *Captain Pugwash* – Yo-ho, me hearties.

The first game against Minchinhampton 1st XV was lost 67–12. However, there was a twenty-minute period in the second half when Mark Pollard scored twice and we could do no wrong. Perhaps the opposition learnt before the game that our sixteen-year-old fullback, Richard, had never played a game of rugby before. Despite this small handicap he played with much spirit (vodka, I think). Bob Goodwin badly strained his groin (no problem there, as he hasn't used that area since 1972). Paul Smith (not Taffy Smith) also injured his area, which resulted in a back bruise stretching from one knee, up over and down again to the other knee. Later comparisons with Desmond Austin's naturally pigmented manhood proved Paul's to be even darker in colour. Many players have since vowed never to eat liverwurst again through fear of reliving this horrendous sight, although it must be said that it would not look out of place stirring a pint of Guinness, providing one was wearing a blazer and club tie.

In the clubhouse after the game, three court trials took place. Norman Blake was charged with the heinous crime of doing a poor impersonation of his son Bingo (star of last year's Irish tour). Despite staggering and singing off-key, he was found guilty and sentenced to twenty years on Devil's Island, which was commuted to standing naked on the table and drinking two pints of beer filtered through his underpants. These were then nailed to the ceiling. Mark Pollard was charged with drunken vandalism and sentenced to be keelhauled. This was commuted to having his Calvin Klein underpants (with designer skid mark no doubt), ripped off and also nailed to the ceiling. This to be followed by standing bollock-naked in the bar for the next three hours. Chris and Brad (Alex's mates from Sittingbourne RFC) were charged with not getting their leg over the night before, despite copping a feel with two local gals. They were both sentenced to be disembowelled on their return from the French Foreign Legion provided in the meantime they had both washed their hands. This was also commuted to wearing each other's clothes for the rest of the day, except for the underpants, whose fate has now started a new Minchinhampton RFC tradition. (Cheaper than Christmas decorations!)

That evening Captain Pugwash took us to a watering hole (and what a hole!) in Stroud. "Left-leg drinking – patches on your middle eye?" We had a quick look at the Hale-Bopp comet and returned to the dry hotel after being poured into taxis.

On the third day, Taffy Smith promised, "Each member of the team will get a screw." This came in the form of Gloucester Prison Warders XV; some were disappointed, but not all.

Chris Naylor was pleased to give his 'bishop' a rest. After all, he laid half the young women of Stroud that weekend and was planning to stay a few extra days to finish the job

Which was commuted to standing naked on the table and drinking two pints of beer filtered through his underpants.

off. The warders borrowed two of our men (can we have them back now, please?) and it looked like being a pushover. But the first half saw Croydon down by only two points. A second-half revival secured a win by 33–23 with tries by Andy Daly (2), Brad Thompson (2) and Bill Coughlan. Richard Cameron converted four.

That evening, our last, was probably spent in a pub somewhere, but unfortunately, despite a full enquiry, no one on our tour has a clear memory. Perhaps it had something to do with the comet or the spaceship following it. Back at the hotel barbed wire was being strung out and the receptionist was removing her Kevlar underwear before painting her naked body with woad and sticking pins in effigies of Andy Salisbury and Richard Cameron. A goat was being sacrificially slaughtered and a demonic incantation recited within a pentagram painted on the front lawn – an event not mentioned in Taffy Smith's 1997 AA Hotel Guide.

After a pub stop on the way back to Croydon, and before you could say, "Well done, Taffy Smith," we were at our final point of call, the Fuller's Beer Spreadeagle in Croydon. We all had a quick one for the road before final departure and hey presto! five hours later most tourists were in the arms of the ones they missed and loved – before they went home.

Those club members who did not attend the tour missed a very good weekend. All the tourists owe a debt of thanks to Roger "Five T's" Entwistle and also to Paul "Taffy" Smith, who took with him on tour a video of Welsh rugby's finest moments. This antique black-and-white footage was very interesting, even though it lasted for only ninety-three seconds.